♥ ♥

Seeds of Love

A Personal and Planetary Transformation

♥ ♥

Seeds of Love

A Personal and Planetary Transformation

Eleonore Koury

Practice Love

♥

When fear arises, practice love
When worry arises, practice love
When uncertainty arises, practice love
When anger arises, practice love

Self love, love of others,
The qualities associated with love -
compassion, understanding,
forgiveness, trust, truth, freedom

The more capacity we have to hold love in
our minds and hearts,

the richer and more brilliant our lives, our
relations and our world.

Practice Love

Contents

Acknowledgements

Thank you Divine Mother/Father
for your Source of strength and love
Thank you to all my guides and teachers
Thank you to my editor and friend Peggy McInerny
Thank you to all that have walked this path with me for
your love, support, encouragement and inspiration:
To my family especially my mother,
father and step parents.
To my partner.
To my friends, colleagues and teachers,
especially Cori Newlander, Kari Colbert, Julie Porter,
Cynthia Landes, Morna Watson, Rheata Rhine, Bob Trask,
Master Yo Hoon, Janette Johnson, Luciana Hardin, Jordan
Allen, the Agape Community, the 12 step community, and
all those unnamed who have been a part of my path,
I am ever grateful.

Introduction

I sit here today feeling called to write but really not sure what to share with you. My journey has been a winding one at best, filled with adventure, challenges, awakenings, pain, deep grief, and deep joy. I am a woman on an unfolding spiritual path, awakening, dancing, and sometimes trudging.

The events in my life that followed 9/11 in the United States were intense and challenging. I was always different, called an anomaly by some, fiery, feisty, spiritual and on the edge. I was also filled with pain, fear, and resentments. 9/11 put a jolt into my system, it felt like the big bang pushing me deeper into awakening. The restlessness I felt for years peaked the year that followed 9/11. Because of my personal history with war, born in Lebanon in 1967 and escaping the war of 1975, I was deeply affected by 9/11 and revisited the wounds of being born into and living through a war.

I had spent five years working in the field of conflict resolution/peer mediation and substance abuse. I began to feel a nudge towards incorporating my spiritual life into my work, yet found it difficult to do in the paradigm I was in. 9/11 sent me deeper into a spiritual search for answers regarding global affairs. I felt disillusioned by our government, disillusioned by the effects we were making as peacemakers and couldn't quite see how educating my students in non-violent methods of dealing with conflict was valid when my government was opting to violence as a way to resolve terrorism. I spent five years telling my students that it made no sense at all to resolve a conflict with violence, that violence begot violence. This mantra had no validity when the adults that many of these students looked to were choosing war. I began searching in alternative holistic venues, and as I did, the hole got deeper and deeper. I was grappling with man and with God. I was experiencing my own unresolved pain and resentment regarding my history with war, the conditioning of religion and culture, sexual abuse, and the years of labor to just get two feet on the ground to build a life.

All my habitual venues of support and spiritual connection were not helping. I felt disconnected and lost. I went to my usual 12 Step meetings and found no solace. I couldn't feel God. I needed more, yet I was truly blocked from receiving anything. I knew that my answers had to come from within me. I was grateful for my mentors, my teachers, my communities, but needed something else.

I do believe that we all go through these cycles, seeking deeper awareness, questioning life, God, and the path. Some of us are pushed into a spiritual quest by life threatening health conditions, accidents, family or relationship break ups. I believe there are many paths to these answers we seek in such times, many paths to God, and many paths to enlightenment. Mine led me to make radical changes in my life. I left a secure job in the mental health field, sold everything and went on a type of sabbatical—no agenda, just open.

The pages that follow relay my search and my findings - A depiction of spirit on a human venture, completing many cycles of human life, dying to the old, awakening, reconnecting with the feminine face of God, uniting in Sacred Marriage with Spirit, unifying in the understanding of the masculine and feminine principles within me, deepening in love, and evolving into Oneness with all.

I feel called to share insights from my journey along with messages I have received from the Divine

Mother/Father. These insights and messages have shaped who I am and continue to be my teachers. I pass on to you that which I find valuable for the individual and the collective.

I make references to yin and yang, which is the creative principle of the Universe. Yin refers to feminine energy and yang refers to masculine energy. Both are present within each of us.

You will read both my interpretations and writings that are a clear relay from a higher source within me. I mark these writings with quotations and indicate it as the Divine Mother/Father. Certainly these sections came through me and reflect my experience.

Take what fits, leave the rest.

As you read these pages, many of you will see and experience your own journey, thoughts and feelings. And so it is with all spiritual journeys, teachings, and writings, for we are one.

♥ ♥
A Journey of Awakening

Awakening

My connection to Spirit deepened in October 2002. Some family members and friends were quite concerned with what I was doing and expressed much doubt. I left a secure income and stable position at a community mental health agency in Los Angeles, sold all of my furniture, and moved into a friend's house in Orange County, California without a plan. I was not unaccustomed to acting against the norm and mystifying friends and family. Yet it was still painful and quite scary to take this leap into the void.

I remember the events that led up to this "change", I felt enormous energy come through during the full cycle of the moon and was compelled to walk or hike in the evenings of the full moon. As I walked in meditation, I listened and received information. At the time I lived in West Los Angeles, CA and often just walked in my neighborhood, always in a circle. It was a form of a labyrinth walk, and coming full circle, I would most always feel comforted and assured with the message I received and the energy I soaked in from the moon. I realize now that this was my way of being with the feminine energy coming from higher dimensions, channeled through the moon. At the time I needed such a powerful natural symbol to tap in to a higher feminine source.

More than anything, 2002 was about BEING. This wasn't too difficult for me. I was the one among my team of colleagues who inspired more play and more opportunities to take the youth we worked with to nature in order to experience the simple gifts of being with themselves and nature. After 9/11, my need to retreat into the wilderness and BE was tremendous. In a way, I realize the event kicked up a well of unresolved pain and grief. I also realize I was carrying, as most women do (and some men), the collective exhaustion of thousands of years of war, rape, abuse and disempowerment.

I spent most of my time available to what the day presented. I had enough money to last three months and so I was free from any work obligations---the period was one of uncovering, discarding and discovering.

I attended Unity Church of Tustin, California, went to their services and attended a variety of workshops that spoke to me. I joined a Yoga Center and explored a variety of body/mind modalities, deepening my yoga practice based on Iyengar principles. I focused on the study of kundalini yoga and experienced an arm of yoga that incorporated movement, breath, chant, and song that added a new dimension to my yoga practice. I spent days upon days in the local wilderness. My second home was Laguna Beach and I was there most days, mainly being with the land. Drifting to what I now know to be lay lines with high frequency energy that called to me. I soaked and soaked and soaked. Often feeling like a pelican perched on a rock.

I had been feeling an inner calling to quest to Crete, Greece. I created a personal pilgrimage that turned into a rite of passage. I ventured to Crete for 21 days. I had researched the Minoan Civilization in which Crete is rich. Mariah Gimbutas in her book "The Goddess Civilization" shares with us through her archeological findings that the Minoans existed for a period of appx 3,000BC to 1,600 BC in a matrilineal society in which the feminine presence was honored and revered. The arts, trade, community, commerce, architecture, etc. were based in the feminine principle of cooperation and harmony. There were no archeological findings of any form of battle materials or structures. This was a civilization that lived in the presence of a feminine deity with a deep connection to the cycles and wisdom of nature and our bodies. Humanity and nature were one. Such a civilization was advanced and it had also created the first sewage system that separated waste so as to not dump it into the ocean. Also, they were the first to create the toilet system. Hence their principles of living were simple, yet evolved and sustainable.

Women carried roles of leadership and along with them men understood and shared in the reverence of feminine power. Gender roles were equal. This was not a matriarchal society but rather matrilineal in which men and women thrived from the reverence and close relation and alignment to the feminine in all. The feminine was in fact the source from which they created and birthed their world.

For as long as I remember I had told family and friends that war was not necessary. Many would reply that humanity has always been in battle and it was in its nature. I replied that was not so. To find archeological fact of a civilization of men and women that had existed without any sign of war for nearly 1,500 years, was tremendous. Now was the time to visit it.

I was drawn to visit the temple sites of this civilization and in many ways it felt like a coming home, a revisit to an era I once lived. On the ancient grounds of the Palace of Knossos and Phaestos I found myself in a deep process. Often times I experienced a regression in which I was clearing past lives. This led to an opportunity to resolve past feelings of anger and resentment at the fall of this civilization and the birth of a warring, competitive, patrilineal society brought on by invasions of the Mycenians and Dorians along with natural disasters such as earthquakes and tsunamis. This was no fault of man alone. Both men and women made choices along, with the divine order of things, that brought this change in civilization about.

This journey accelerated the process of clearing, healing and awakening for me, an ongoing process. I deepened in the process of self-forgiveness and forgiveness of the tides of civilization. I experienced more clarity and began to see the world around me from a new perspective. I returned with a sense of service and a deeper awareness of my purpose in this life – a time to complete many lives, to heal, forgive and awaken to my divinity and the divinity of the world.

After several weeks of processing the journey and still having no idea what line of work to enter, I started to share my experience with many others as it came time to do so. But it was difficult to relay. I had cleared deep levels of karma and had tapped into a Source within me that wanted to express itself, but did not know how. I had a renewed vision of a world as a sacred whole. That if it once existed, it could again, and now in a renewed, enlightened way.

I began to see that in fact humanity had cut itself off from its Source. It had cut itself off from the simple truth that we are one. One with nature, one with the Divine Mother/Father, and one with each other.

I sought out people and communities that reflected this renewed vision and began to create my own through Sacred Ventures, leading day journeys in local canyons to reconnect participants with the healing and awakening qualities of nature.

I was guided to the healing arts to expand my awareness and deepen my own personal healing of body, mind and spirit. I was eventually led back to Los Angeles to share my insights and awareness. I returned to the environment I could not tolerate and found a new sense of inner peace and stillness that was not impacted by the energy of the city. I had a keen awareness of who and what to relate to and connect with. My life for several years was focused inward. Many of my past relationships dissolved and my experience and journey to Greece began to move more towards a journey within.

This led me to the Agape International Spiritual Center and expanded experiences of the healing arts. Through receptionist work at the Well Being Center at Agape, I absorbed a variety of healing modalities and continued my personal healing while in service to others.

Yearly Pilgrimage

I found a new pattern and ritual had embedded itself in my psyche after my pilgrimage to Crete. It became important each year to go on a quest -- whether for a day, a week or a month -- as part of connecting to nature, to myself and to Spirit. I discovered that my primary relationship was with Spirit and these yearly or biannual quests allowed me to strengthen my connection. Though these quests began in distant regions, I now find they can occur anywhere. All that is needed is my intention and the Universe provides the conditions and situation that suits the time. I find the more I let go of it having to look a certain way, the more the quest naturally arises out of life. In fact now the Universe doesn't wait for me to plan a journey, it will create one when I am being called, and I find myself questing.

I continued my quest the following year at Molokai, Hawaii, on a week-long retreat that prepared me for 36 hours in the wilderness. In stillness I awakened subtly to a deeper awareness of the divine feminine/ the Great Mother. In the middle of the night, awakened by some fear and uncertainty, these feelings were then washed over completely by this presence. All around me and within me I felt her. She was there and it was safe. She was within me and I was in her. All of a sudden the wilderness was no longer something outside of me to fear or challenge and be challenged by, but rather a powerful force that was also gentle and loving. Earth took on a new level of reality. She was alive and in her was the essence and presence of the Divine Mother. I felt held and nourished in body, mind and spirit. I felt plugged in to my Source and I felt one with her.

At the time I wasn't fully clear about what had occurred. I knew something had shifted within, and in time would be revealed. It isn't until now, as I write this, that I fully understand the scope of what occurred. And that in me the spark of the Christ consciousness was awakening. And today, as so many around the world, the feminine face of Christ moves and breathes through me, as me, each moment, each day.

Attunement to Reiki

When I returned home from my quest in Molokai I was led to become attuned to Reiki and found a deepening of my external experiences in Crete and Hawaii. What I experienced in these regions began to open and awaken more deeply from within. As I worked with Reiki I experienced its qualities of love, compassion, healing, abundance, and creativity as a reflection of the divine feminine awakening within me. I was called to work on others and began one on one sessions, eventually leading to group classes which I began to teach. The process of teaching for me was one of awakening in others their divine nature and the essence of the feminine to flow through them, embracing and integrating body, mind and spirit for both men and women.

My work has evolved as have I, clearing and deepening. Some awaken to their divine nature and it is an instant and they are free of the separation, others awaken more gradually, allowing the Higher Self to lead. I believe this process is happening to many of us, and the re-awakening of the feminine is emerging in all of us, men and women.

For thousands of years we have lived asleep to the equality of both principles, the very creative element of the Universe. The yin and yang. Hence the great imbalance we suffer in countless illnesses and diseases in humanity and society.

The time has come for the *Great Balance* and *Great Ascension* to occur. Spirit and matter no longer separated.

Body, mind and spirit united, a great peace and deep understanding of the divine feminine in harmony and equality with the divine masculine.

We are all awakening and ascending. Some slowly, some quickly. It will occur in all of us and to our planet earth.

My Year of Celibacy

In August 2005, a year after my Molokai quest I received this very clear guidance from my guides to go into a year of celibacy, while sitting under a tree in Laguna Beach at Hysler Park. "We want you to spend time in celibacy." A few days later the exact time became clear. I was asked to stay celibate for one year. I was not happy about this. I had spent two years without a relationship and had experienced a lot of frustration at being alone, I had such a deep craving to meet my mate, my partner on this path.

At first it was easy, I surrendered. By the holiday season and in the New Year I was preparing to date. I had almost forgotten about my commitment. I had just finished manifesting a new car and so wanted to continue creating, a mate was next in my mind. It was time, in my mind, I was tired of being alone. I had done my work for God's sake; done everything I'd been asked.

Then a new client referred by an existing client came into my office and began sharing that she was committing to a year of celibacy. The light went off. Almost like a tap on my head. And that's all it took, I surrendered and re-committed. There were temptations and distractions. I found it easy to abandon my Self and Spirit and our commitment. Then there was the grief, so much grief as I had visioned that I would do this work with a partner. I wanted to share this life and the day to day affairs with another and was tired of waiting. It wasn't until the end of my period of celibacy that I began to understand, but not entirely until its completion. The period of celibacy was just the foundation, for my Kundalini energy (sexual/spiritual energy) to find its root in Spirit.

I found that at points during the celibacy, I felt my energy like I had never felt it before. I was celibate both with myself and with others. When sexual energy rose it was channeled into creation. I focused the energy into my work and allowed it to reveal other avenues within. I experienced the sacredness of my sexual energy -- it was powerful, it was creation, when aligned with Spirit it created and it healed. My kundalini was rising, opening and awakening. The depth of my experience in relationships and in my work took on a new level. I experienced a reservoir in me no one had ever told me about. I experienced this power: the shakti, the base of the kundalini, the creatrix within me.

I feel this more and more now.

I live in a culture where women are free. And with that freedom, we are creating and healing and mobilizing to create a better world for ourselves on this earth and for generations to come. And yet my sense is there is a level of that freedom we have yet to tap into. It is connected to our kundalini energy, our life force, and its capacity to rise to higher levels of consciousness.

This higher level of consciousness is the gateway to a new reality and awareness of our life force energy and its union with our Higher Self. Rather than being ruled by our self-centered desires, we are guided by our Higher Self and a higher presence. This does not mean that life is devoid of pleasure. Quite the contrary, we experience pleasure with a deeper and truer sense. It is more satisfying and fulfilling. It lacks the addictive quality because it is in line with our deeper awareness and therefore there is a knowing when to let go and an aligning with a higher will.

Partnership

My celibacy came to a conclusion in August of 2006 and I began to date and open to my higher mate. This led me to a sacred partnership with a beautiful man. I believe that my journey led me to this experience. The year of celibacy and my time in sacred union with Spirit set a foundation so that when uneasiness emerges in my relationship with my partner, my connection within is present and I eventually return to that reservoir. The sacredness I experienced through my celibacy is now experienced in my intimate relationship with my partner. Our intimacy fosters healing, evolution and deepens my experience of, and union with the divine.

I was challenged early on in my relationship because I unconsciously created an expectation during my time in celibacy and on pilgrimage that my mate would mirror my relationship with Spirit. In many ways he did reflect the beauty of my primary relationship however, I was challenged when he revealed his issues and we were faced with our differences and our power struggle. I was confronted with my personal pain body and ego and the collective female pain body and ego. I was also faced with a mate who presented his personal pain body and ego and represented the collective male pain body and ego. As our relationship deepened, I found myself with a partner who was my teacher in patience compassion, love, and truth. I found that my process during celibacy was continuing in partnership.

This partnership led to a deepening of my connection within, assisting me in clearing false concepts of partnership and the role of a mate. Through the combination of my time in celibacy and my time in partnership, I found myself continually clearing outmoded concepts and opening to a true partnership with Spirit, myself, and my mate. I found that some of the healing and awakening work I did solo could only really complete in partnership. I continually faced the old patterns of mistaking my source of peace, joy, and fulfillment to come from a relationship. This illusion is passed down to us on a DNA level. It is in facing the death of that idea that I found myself reborn in truth. Fulfillment comes from my right relationship with myself and Spirit, and my partner supports those relationships. Whenever I mistake my partner as my source of peace and joy, I am doomed to misery and suffering. But when I move through the illusion and connect to my true Source, I find great freedom.

It is a result of our individual and joint relationship with Spirit, and our communication, that our partnership is able to foster intimacy, healing and evolution, transcending the ego and healing the pain body. Our shared spiritual connection supports us through our challenges. Sacred sex and periods of celibacy deepens that spiritual connection and supports our growth individually and as a couple.

I believe it is our personal spiritual practice, along with our combined practice of prayer, meditation, and ceremony that strengthens our relationship and keeps us together through difficult patches. I believe it is divine presence that helps us transcend our egos and allows our love to shine through. I believe it is divine love that brought us together and it is divine love that keeps us together for as long as it is in our highest good.

♥ ♥
Messages from the Divine Mother/Father

God the Mother

Tonight I sit and write on the eve of a beautiful full moon after hearing and watching a powerful group of Asian drummers. As we approach the anniversary of September 11, I feel the fire coming through and the power of the feminine calling out – "write, write, tell them I am here. Tell them the time is now, tell them to listen, Be Still and Know that I AM. It is time, the feminine face of Christ/God is ready to reveal Herself and is coming through, receive Her."

As young girls and boys we were cut off from our very source, raised in a predominantly male culture with a male God, removed from us and judgmental. Our source of freedom, of rest, of ease, and of peace, our source of well-being and of prosperity. Many of us were not raised in a manner that allowed us to see the reality that God is also our Mother, that she is within us all and we are within her. She is abundant and beautiful and powerful and she is the source of all, as is the Father.

The words from the Agape Choir ring out: "Mother Father God, how great thou art, how infinite, how wonderful."

This presence of the divine is within me, is me and is all around me. She comforts, consoles, heals. He guides, encourages, supports. It loves, challenges, illuminates. And it tells us there is nothing, absolutely nothing, you have to do to receive these gifts. Just open to the message: "You are deeply loved."

The Quickening Quickens

It is October 2006 and the message of the Divine Mother is coming to Agape through Sharon McErlane's Grandmothers Gatherings (www.grandmothersspeak.com) and Marabi Devi. There is a strong Mother presence this week. I feel her moving through me and edging me forward. I surrender and open.

I am grateful.

I trust.

I know all my needs are taken care of, despite outward appearances. The ego and lower vibrations are also strong this week -- I feel it in the outer world. It's interesting, I'm having a different experience in my inner world. Less reactive, more observant.

It is the anniversary of my second year at Molokai, Hawaii, during which I served participants preparing for their quests. I am reminded of the powerful lessons I learned and feel a refinement of the tools I learned there. I was taken to the edge through my time in service and pushed into being fully in the moment, letting go of false ideas and agendas. It was powerful cleansing of the ego.

I woke this morning in a dream, three obese people were in my car but there wasn't enough room for me. It felt like I'd taken on passengers that don't belong in my life. So there is more clearing off of clutter and distractions.

It is Fall, a time to clear and cleanse. Cleansing and releasing what no longer serves, making room to plant the seeds in the dark soil of winter to take fruit in the spring and summer.

As the feminine is embraced, the body is honored and its wisdom understood. So too are the seasons and cycles of the earth. Each season with its purpose, facilitating the process of renewal – life, death and rebirth. A continuous cyclical evolutionary process. A reflection of the Christ consciousness within.

"Let things fall off that need to.

Let things come in that need to.

Trust me.

I've got you.

I love you."

Infusion of the Feminine

The energy of the Divine Mother is strong in me now. It is May 2007. I have moved my healing practice into a new space, The Healing Center. My business partner and I were blessed with a center of our own. We have dedicated the center to the Divine Mother and to the healing and awakening that is happening on this planet.

After teaching a Reiki Master class and hosting the first Grandmothers Gathering here, I feel a hunger to retreat and write. I find the evolutionary process of my spiritual path interesting. It began with a strong connection to and inspiration from Jesus. This connection then awakened the rightful role of Mary Magdalene and her true identity as the feminine face of Christ. And that connection moved me to unite with Spirit, as the Beloved, without gender, one Source. I am awakening to all aspects of the divine, and the important role of the Divine Mother in the Oneness:

"I am everywhere!! There is no where I AM not." The Great Mother is anchoring on earth in a renewed way. We revered her in Neolithic times. We understood her well. We understood the laws of creation and manifestation.

We then needed to divert the feminine with strong masculine energy in order to take our creations around the globe and connect materially, physically.

Now it is time to balance those energies, infusing more feminine – depth, softness, rest, nurturance, containment – into our experience of God, Spirit, Universal Consciousness, etc.

"People will resist the change.

They will resist, they resist now. It is not wanted by many, yet wanted by many.

No wrong has been done.

It is a time of evolution and balancing. That is all.

It is time for more love.

I come now to assist the planet in evolving.

You must tell them to be at peace. To trust. To go within. You must tell them that all their needs are met. Keep it simple. Do daily prayer and meditation."

The Great Mother awakens in our consciousness at this time to comfort, to heal us, to cradle us and to guide us. She tells us we are precious emanations of the light. She tells us to remember. She calls us home.

"Many will resist, it is inevitable.

Do not be distracted by the affairs of the world. There will be calamity, it is part of the resistance. Stay centered in the light of your heart. Follow your inner guidance and stay connected to your brothers and sisters through authentic love.

Love will reside on this planet and will have its way with ALL.

Love will heal everything.

Like a wave, it will wash over all wounds, all the separation, ALL.

I am sending many at this time to come to your aid, to assist you in this transition. I send many rays, many beings of light, many avatars, saints and enlightened ones. I call out to many at this time. Many have answered and are being prepared to guide you at this time on this plane. Go to the healers and teachers you feel guided to. Listen, learn, clear your house out, clear your affairs. Forgive, let go, and love. Do whatever you need to do to be in Love. That is your protection and your guide for everything. It is simple.

I speak through many at this time. Do not become attached to any. They are merely guides and reflections of my light and love for you. You can hear me and receive me directly I am in your *heart*, where I have always been. Clear your heart, honor and heal your pain, release resentments, fears, and worries. I am with you. Always, in all ways. I am one with the Father, I am the Mother. Your Eternal Mother and I Love You.

I want nothing from you.

I only want that you listen to and receive me.

Open your hearts.

Trust your inner guidance; most of all, have faith in love.

It will heal all your wounds, all your concerns. Love only wants the best for you and is constantly operating in your highest good. Love is the glue of the universe.

Simplify, clear and trust. You are in the arms of the Great Mother."

The Mother Wants to Be Known

Things are quiet these days. Mother seems to have cleared my calendar. It's often hard to trust the direction, as so many doubts arise. Then there is this wave of peace. Oh my goodness, it is intense. This feeling that all is well. It's familiar, yet unfamiliar. It's a feeling of being and living in higher dimensions. A space where all your needs are met -- everything, physical, mental, emotional, financial, ethereal. There is no doubt or fear.

In these higher dimensions, Mother is known and revered (higher meaning true, clear, open, simple). There is no separation. You feel completely cradled by her, in her bosom, in her land. Everything is beautiful. The colors are vibrant and amazing: the smells, the tastes, I can't quite describe it. And yet I find it fascinating that I am on earth, yet I move in and out of different fields of consciousness, different dimensions. This process began in 2001, the acceleration of my awakening. My reality began to alter radically, I began to awaken to the reality that I am a multidimensional being living in a multidimensional universe. At first this realization was difficult to deal with. Each jump or shift in dimension would knock my socks off and rock my world. Now the process is easier, smoother.

I recognize that the Divine Mother is going to continue sending energy and messages through me more clearly.

It's really quite simple: we are all tapped in. As we are aligned, listening and conversing with her.

I feel her grace now. Sometimes it gets shaken, mostly when I give power to someone or something outside of me.

I would say what deepened my connection to the Divine Mother was my quest on the hills of Molokai when I first felt her as a field of energy and a source all around me. The Reiki attunements then allowed me to deepen the awareness that she is within me and I am within her. I then spent several years in close relationship with my natal mother. Experiencing the love of the Mother through her, unconditional and constant.

Through my journeys and inner teachings I began to awaken to the vastness of the Mother.

We have for a long time tapped into the energy of the Father, which is also everywhere and within. I don't know that we have quite awakened to the reality that the Mother is one with Father. Yin and yang. The basic energy of the universe. It is one. It cannot separate. She is vast everywhere and all loving. She is God the Mother. And She wishes to be known.

She tells you that you are connected to the Source of all. There is no separation. All you need is available to you. It does not need some fancy ritual or prayer or ceremony. She tells you these things help connect you to her however, they are not necessary. She is right here. No separation. And she is one with God the Father.

It is time for both to be fully known on this earth plane. They are one. As we all are.

Everything is Buoyant

We are held in a field of Love and it is fluid, it is water. It is the womb. We are held by the womb of the Mother, the feminine principle of the universe. We have forgotten this truth. In the arms of the Mother we are in a constant state of love and peace. All of our needs are taken care of. There is no fear, there is no effort. Life is ease and grace. That is the nature of it. No efforting. Simply being, flowing, and living.

This experience of life is foreign to many of us.

The laws in which we have been operating are in large part based on a yang/masculine paradigm. The masculine principle is crucial in assisting us to move forward and take action. However, we are now moving into a new paradigm, the union of the masculine and feminine, it is the sacred union, the sacred marriage. It's an equal dance. And that is what it is, a dance. The yin/yang dance of the great oneness. Body and matter uniting with mind and spirit.

We need a period of time immersed in feminine energy to restore the imbalance of the last several millennia. We will live in the buoyancy of the feminine and restore our balance. We will honor our bodies and the body of the earth. The masculine within us - the mind, spirit, action aspect of ourselves - will support the feminine at this time. It will pass the leadership role to the feminine. The feminine will lead, honoring the body and creating with love, light, openness, and freedom. Guiding in a new paradigm based in *ease and grace, healing, abundance, cooperation, and nurturance.*

The masculine in each of us will supply the action for the feminine in all of us to act on behalf of the higher good and anchor this new paradigm of harmony, love and truth, of being. A shift, in which doing is born from being, from resting like a baby in the arms of the Great Mother/Father. This process reminds me of Anne Geddes photographs -- images of newborn infants in complete state of rest, completely surrendered, trusting, fully at peace, surrounded by love and light.

"Many will be challenged by this new way, because it requires very little. This will be difficult for people. They will take many unnecessary actions. This will create despair and anxiety. They will keep themselves busy so as to not feel the openness and vastness that I am and to realize that I am carrying them and sustaining them. It will take them awhile to fully trust that the Mother can support them fully and that She is one with the Father. They will fear the rest. They will resist it. They will fear the lack of action and the call to rest in the divine. Mostly they will resist the feminine energy in them and in the world. Masculine energy has become a drug for many.

Tell them to not be afraid, that I am here with them, in them and guiding them, that I have sent many to assist them in this transition, that the Mother/Father is with them and supporting in this transition. Tell them that I love them, always have, always will. Tell them all their needs are met, and everything, everything, is working for their higher good."

Compassion

Mother and the angelic realm want you to know that they see the level of pain and suffering many of you have endured on this plane.

"We know how painful it has been. Many of you suffer from physical challenges, others from mental challenges, and others, deep emotional scarring.

We know the anguish you have walked with. We know the loneliness you have endured and the suffering that has resulted for so many of you leaving you feeling isolated and cut off from the Source that nourishes you and consoles you and cradles you.

These scars that so many have endured on a soul level can be difficult to heal and can create years of anguish and embedded patterning. Many of you seek to understand why such things happen, many are taught that it is your karmic cycles. I, your Divine Mother, say to you that it does not matter. I notice not your karma or your reasons. Today I am present with you and holding you and cradling you telling you I am sorry you have endured so much. I am sorry the pain has been so heavy and for so long.

Please keep in your heart the assurance that the divine is working tirelessly to help heal the wounds of the human soul and your planet earth.

We are infusing divine love into your planet continuously, assisting the movement out of old patterns and pain.

The collective body of your planet has much to heal. We are holding the space for that healing and aiding the process.

A parasite is clearing from your field. A dis-ease, if you will, of the human spirit and of the planet earth. She and you are healing and renewing.

So rest in us, rest, do not resist the changes and know that we are with you."

I Will Heal All

The Divine Mother comes to tell us that she will heal all of our wounds. She will flow in all of our dark corners. She will leave no rock unturned. She will shine the light on and will love every ache, every hurt, every pain. Just like a mother attends to a young child's wound.

She comes at this time to tell us that she is here to comfort, to console, to cradle. We HAVE nothing to DO. Merely to receive.

"Let ME IN.

I will support you in all ways. I will not take away from you your freedom, your will. Rather, I will give you more freedom and much, much ease.

Trust me.

I am Everywhere. I am the food you eat. I am the air you breathe that sustains your life. I am the ground you walk on. I am everywhere.

Why do you fear? Or forget? I carry you.

I am the one that cradles you at night while you sleep. I am the feather you feel at your cheek. I am the kisses and the sweetness that comes through the ether. I AM LOVE.

Let me love you. Feel my love. Hear that all is well. All your needs are met in Me. Lean into me and align to your unlimited source. My love is your strength."

The Feminine in Harmony with Masculine

Today the energy coming through me is Masculine. There is a new moon and the action energy is strong. The waning moon always pulls you back into the cave for rest and restoration, pulling you in to the feminine, into the depth, the wisdom. The period at the new moon to the waxing and full moon is full of young renewed energy, yang, outward, action-oriented energy.

Both energies are so crucial. The sacred dance of yin and yang energies of the universe the great oneness.

Yesterday, while walking on the Marina peninsula, I saw pelicans flying in pairs in such perfect harmony. Carrying the wind in their wings, flowing with the rhythms of the winds vibration and in harmony with each other. It was truly beautiful to watch, to witness nature's majestic ways.

As I watched the pelicans I saw the sacred dance, the beautiful dance of partnership, and I was reminded of the sacred dance of the feminine and masculine energies, both within us and in our partnerships. We individually carry these energies, sometimes more on one side than the other. But similarly to the earth's current rebalancing, we too, are rebalancing individually. It seems there is a fine art of honoring the feminine cycles in our individual lives and the feminine cycles of the earth, as well as honoring the masculine cycles.

It appears that nature's intelligence is in perfect balance. Our task is to stay in harmony with this balance. Not to get too ahead of it or too behind it. That is, not too ahead of the feminine energy and not too behind the masculine energy.

In our world, and individually, we are currently saturated in the masculine energy. It has gone to the extreme, causing us to run around like mad people. We, as a collective unit are out of sync with the feminine cycle and the power of depth, rest and containing. We are enamored with quick, fast, glitzy.

We need to honor more feminine time. Even in new cycles of action, we must temper with resting, being...flowing with them, not spinning out with new energy.

The Mother will guide us with our evolution. She will show us individually how to hold the masculine energy to allow it to support our growth. She will guide us to evolve and mature, tempering our pleasures, deepening them, savoring them and truly enjoying them.

Bring the new energies into your being and rest in their fullness. Let them go deep within you. Ask the Mother to guide you in their use, ask her for wisdom. This will allow for deeper experiences in life instead of the quick flash that leads to a thirst that is never quenched.

She will help you anchor masculine energy and work with it to move you forward and evolve, rather than be driven by it and spin out into delusion and burn out.

Have fun playing, rest in the Divine Mother, and allow her to guide you.

Your Work is not Your Source; I Am

"For far too long people have mistaken their work as their source -- source of everything, money, security, esteem, you name it.

It is a false reality, the illusion of the divine play. Your work is a result of your connection to Spirit. Spirit is your ultimate security, esteem, prosperity. People do not bring it to you. I do, it comes from within you. The outer is a reflection of the inner. People and work come and go, like waves in the ocean.

I do not come and go. I am constant. I am always. I am here. Always. Consistent. Available. Present. Solid. I AM.

Ultimately, that is all that matters. Your connection to Me. To your Source. To the Divine.

This Source also comes through others, the flicker of hope, the light and love in your partner's eyes, the support of a friend. This is the divine, the true nature of the Universe, the connective web of life.

Have faith and trust in this Source. Do not attach to people, places and things. Surrender to the Higher Good that is their Source.

Truly I tell you this: where there is any calamity, misuse, or disaster, I am the comfort, the counsel, the healing elixir. Wherever there is celebration, jubilation, delight, victory, I am there rejoicing, celebrating, embracing.

Connect with Me first and the rest will come. Let go of your attachment to people, places, and things – in that lies your freedom.

Freedom lives in aligning with the divine first. You are then broken of the illusion and delusion of what is "needed" to live joyfully. You are then fully immersed in joy and peace. All your needs are met. All.

So release. Let go. Follow your inner deep guidance. Align with the divine and its joys and pleasures will come to you easily and effortlessly, as they will leave easily and effortlessly.

Surrender to the flow, to the waves of constant change, to bliss."

Be patient with yourself as you adopt these concepts. I have found it challenging to truly live with the divine as my Source and not mistake the gifts that come from my Source as the Source. This can become an especially difficult trap when we mistake someone we love or an experience we enjoy as the Source. We want to hang on so tightly and keep it.

Loss can be a difficult thing to heal and release. But loss is a part of life, it is part of the creative force of the universe, expanding and contracting. Give yourself the love and gentleness to let go and find the freedom in your relationship with your Source, knowing that it is always working towards your highest good. As things or people fall away there is always, always Divine Presence, which is love.

Be patient, with yourself and with the process, forgive yourself and others and allow your heart to remain open.

I remember the words of my partner's spiritual teacher that "nothing is ever lost." It is true. We take with us all the experiences and all the love we have shared. Though people, places or things may change, the love that is experienced and shared remains.

Comfort in Challenging Times and in Good Times

"My dear ones know that I am with you. I am everywhere. I am in your banks, your grocers, your post offices, your gas stations. I am in the ocean, in the mountains, in the computer that you write on. I am everywhere. I am the air you breathe. I am the wind and I am the sunset. I am the moon and the night sky. I am all around you. I am in you, I am the wisdom of your body. Trust me.

I am everywhere. I know your heart, dear ones. I know your longings. I hear your cries. And I answer. I answer. I answer. You may not receive my answer in the way you expect. But know that I always answer. Know that the universe is always working for your higher good. Life is always repairing itself. Humanity is designed to heal itself just as the earth is. Allow both to heal. Go with the rumblings and the shakings, dance with it. It may not appear to make sense at times, it may appear that it keeps getting worse…stay with the new world, stay with the truth and the vision. And you shall create it.

Yours is to learn how to dance with the changes. Flow with them. Don't push. Don't fight. Go with the rhythms of your life. Go with the ups and the downs. Like the waves in the ocean, sometimes the tide is high and ferocious, sometimes calm and serene. This is the tide of life. Relax, be at ease. Flow with it. Don't push. Don't resist. Flow with it. I am there holding you and comforting you during the challenging waters and I am there laughing and dancing with you in the good times."

The Divine Mother tells us, "I am here for you, speak my name, men and women. Call on Me, call on My graces and rest in My bosom. I am here at this time to aid the world in her healing and all her people. Let go of your resistance and rest. I heal all with my Love. Nothing else. It's really pretty simple it's what the saints and avatars have realized over the ages.

Speak to me consistently. My love is ageless and limitless. Prayer is merely communing/communicating with me, aligning with me. Commune with me often to bring me into your everyday affairs -- morning, noon and night. And trust that I am taking care of all the details. My love is the glue. Stay in the field of love for all and it will be taken care of."

Facets of the Divine Mother

The Divine Mother appears to me often these days, I feel her presence and see her luminous Light within me. It is a bit overwhelming at times. Sometimes I can only catch a glimpse, sometimes I catch the whole image and feel consumed by her.

Mother Mary was the embodiment of the Divine Mother on this earth plane. Often I will experience her image and often the image changes shapes and forms. This form takes on a more general image of the sacred mother, or the benevolent mother. Sometimes she comes in the image of Mary of Guadalupe of the Catholic tradition and sometimes beyond any tradition or religion. All her forms represent the Great Mother and her love.

The Great Mother can also take the form of the dark goddess. She will stir in the depth of my being, and shake off whatever is not useful. I experience her as a force of change, a destroyer of what is no longer useful and transformer into the new. This facet of the Divine Mother is known as Kali.

We can construct a limited image of the Great Mother, neglecting to see all facets, the depth and the dark as well as the lightness and warmth. We see this with the role of Mary Magdalene at the time of Jesus. Mary Magdalene represented the dark Madonna embodying the Divine Mother in her raw essence – true, sensual, passionate, a shaman, healer, minister, and more.

All are facets of the Divine Mother -- nurturer, caregiver, creator, destroyer, healer and more.

I remember my Spirit Quest in the Wilderness of Molokai, Hawaii -- the three-year anniversary this month of May. On the eve of my quest, under the night sky I went through layers of my ego, in and out of fear and safety. Then I awoke for no particular reason, but remember looking up at the night sky and feeling this overwhelming awareness that I was ok and fully enveloped by a loving presence I could not quite describe. It was female in nature, and I was enveloped in its safe presence. It was all around me and was awakening within me. I was safe in my body and in the body of the earth.

I realize now that it was God the Mother. But at the time I was so hooked into Christ the male Jesus, and the pursuit of connecting with him that I didn't quite recognize that the thing I was seeking had in fact revealed itself.

When I returned from the quest I knew something had happened, but I didn't know what. I knew something had planted and would emerge in its right time. Now the time seems to have come.

I recall that the leader of the quest, asked me what had happened to me overnight.

I didn't have an answer to his question. I told him that I knew something happened, something deep within me had awakened and shifted, but that I had no words for it and could not quite explain it.

Now it is being revealed. The Christ I was seeking was in me. As my spiritual guide and therapist of the time had told me, the Jesus I was seeking was in me. The feminine face of Christ was awakening in me and is now moving through me. It takes the form of the divine feminine, the divine masculine, of God the Mother/Father.

It speaks through me and moves as me when I open to it and when It wants to.

"I am here at this time for the great change that is happening on this planet to awaken all to the reality of the great oneness that carries within it the great man/ woman, yin/yang, feminine/masculine principle. For far too long now you have carried the weight of the male god and created a world in this structure. Disconnecting from your inner wisdom and your connection to the divinity of your body temple. This is out of balance and must shift now. I am here to bring this shift about.

Many will speak my words and the one who writes this book speaks my words and lives my truth. She shares with you a glimpse of the cosmic reality. She opens to my energy and anchors the divine feminine. Hear her words, find what resonates for you and listen to me within you. As I speak through her so I also speak through you. I am available to you all. I am the still small voice within you that comforts you and soothes the pain. I am the one that carries you and cradles you. You have forgotten me. I am the Great Mother. The Father and I call you today to awaken you to the reality that we are one and yet we are two distinct energies -- unique and individual as each of you are emanations of this oneness.

The very part of you that is feminine has been buried for centuries. It is time for her emergence and her integration in you individually and in your world. She is the yin principle. She is flesh, deep, dark, alive. She is pleasure, creativity, nurturance, she holds and contains. Allow her to emerge in you, man or woman."

Mary Magdalene did not have the same recognition as Jesus and the patriarchy cut the equal partnership out. Their union was meant to fulfill the equal dance of the feminine and masculine, the divine united.

So the call strengthens, the empowerment of the feminine all around the world, bringing the feminine face of Christ (or Buddha) and God the Mother to the forefront.

The Matrix of the divine feminine -- Sophia, Mary, Quan Yin, Lakshmi, Kali, etc. -- is emanating in us. Shining her face in all of us, stepping forward like a force of lightning. It is time.

She calls us now. And she awaits our response and offers us repose in her bosom.

Mary said to her disciples, "You are midwives of the Mother Spirit and you are meant to labor with Her in the harvest of souls. Yet do not grasp on to the fruit of your labors, for it is She who accomplishes everything and to whom all good fruits belong."

Mary said, " No one will know the Living Father apart from the Mother, for it is She who shows us the face of our Father."

St Mary Magdalene, The Gnostic Tradition of the Holy Bride, Tau Malachi

Trust in Your Union with the Mother

"Tell them to lean in to me and know all is well. I am taking care of all your needs. I am real, not a figment of your imagination. I am the Great Mother that you have forgotten. I am here and very much alive and will be even more so through your belief and trust in me.

As in any partnership your trust is key to our union and communion. I will love you and give to you no matter what you do. However, your trust in me increases the field of energy between us and the flow of grace in your existence on this plane.

You can live without trust or belief but you will experience suffering and discord. Your trust and belief neutralize the discord and creates a fluid union, a bridge between us. It is through that bridge that I communicate to you and that you listen to me, and that you communicate to me and I listen to you -- oh yes, my dear ones, I DO LISTEN to you, I hear, feel, and see every word, every thought, every emotion.

Trust me, all is really truly well and in your highest good."

The Old is Dying into the New

I ventured on my 2007 quest in May, the month of the Mother. The Mother is in fact the bearer of all of life. It is through her that the manifest world is realized. She is the creatrix from which all life comes.

And so it is my first day of my quest of 2007 at Warner Springs Ranch in San Diego, California. I have a headache. I've been resisting being alone this year because this energy feels so intense. It is coming into me and awakening in me.

As I honor this time of retreat, I embrace the feminine, honoring my body, resting my mind, simply being. Warner Springs is one of the many beautiful places around the world with natural hot springs. Water symbolizes the feminine, and so as I dipped into the mineral springs I felt the sacred communion of my body with the warm waters. Almost like a babe in the womb. I also felt like my body symbolized the earth as she soaked in the womb of the Great Mother. As I soaked, I felt the core of my being and all its circuits, organs, muscles, and tissue nourished. I also felt as if the healing of my body was impacting the healing of Mother Earth and all humanity. It is a reality that as we heal ourselves, as insignificant as it may seem, we are healing the collective and the earth.

I was in ceremony, a sacred dip, like a baptism. As I united with the waters, I saw the feminine returning to our planet earth. I saw the earth's grid infused with healing light (similar to the energy lines(meridians) and centers(chakras) of a human being, the earth also has vortexes and ley lines known as the earth's grid.)

I saw the great awakening of the feminine body in us all. The honoring of the sacred feminine in man and woman. A return in a renewed way of the indigenous ways and a new awakening of the divinity of our bodies.

I begin to see the opportunity to be of service and to renew in my connection to Spirit. This is a powerful time in our world. I feel it strongly now and see the reason for being on quest alone.

I communicated with my guides "I am present and ready for my quest, please guide me."

They replied, "Crow Feather (one of my guides) is here with you along with Archangel Michael. Worry not my dear one, we are all around you and sending guidance from all places. You are fully protected and blessed. We are grateful that you have come out at this time to commune with the divine and to write."

And so I begin to settle into my journey. As evening approached fear began to rise due to an uncomfortable experience with one of the residents of the Ranch.

Strangely enough many of us are born into fear. Isn't that odd. We come from love and awaken to a reality filled with fear and separation. How and why that occurred is still a riddle to me. There are many explanations, much of it is a mystery.

As I sit here in my cabin at Warner Springs after a sleepless night I realize at a deeper level that most of the time we are living an illusion. That in fact all is truly good and safe. Love is all around us. Yet we are constantly receiving external stimulation from other people's experiences or triggered into our old experiences. This leads to separation from ourselves, our bodies and the present moment.

After my first day and night I feel a bit disturbed as if I am clearing something. I awoke with disturbance in my field triggered into childhood memories of having my energy and body invaded and rarely feeling safe in my space.

Though I have quested and traveled alone to other regions, and in the wilderness I find myself still clearing the illusion that I am not safe. I suppose this belief has been true for a long time due to the paradigm in which we live. But today the safety comes from within and is the right of every woman, man and child. Women do not need to be protected, nor do they need to be manly to protect themselves or be walled off. Protection is the reality we are creating. It is a world of wisdom, honor, and grace. Therefore men and women can walk in integrity and women are able to fully carry the feminine energy and be safe.

As women, it is time for us to be free in our world and live freely in body and mind. It is time for that separation to dissolve. It is also time for us to take responsibility for our space and our feminine energy. It is crucial that we clear what blocks us from fully stepping into our feminine power.

So many women struggle with autonomy in partnership, so many seek fulfillment through their mate. They also confuse their mate with their Higher Source and often abandon their connection to that Source for partnership. There is a way to do both, to live in harmony and alignment with their mate and with one's Source. It is time for balanced partnerships in which we are mutually present, available and supportive. Rather than a source of obligation and dependence, we are able to empower each other and enable each others growth.

When we are traumatized and our experience of the world is one of violation, pain and separation, we instinctively shut down. We cut ourselves off from our Source. We cut off our senses and our connection to our bodies so as to not feel the pain, the fear, the low vibrations that throw us off balance. We mistrust ourselves and our connection within, making it scary to live in silence, trusting ourselves and our inner guidance.

Shutting ourselves off from our body's wisdom and our Source leads to a low level of energy for life. We become victims of our world. We stop creating our world and instead live a life of reacting to the world created around us.

As we heal ourselves, we begin to awaken and evolve. We reconnect with ourselves, our bodies and the present moment. This allows us to create responsibly with our energy. We are then able to make wise choices and stop reacting to each other and our world.

Moving out of reacting into consciously acting, we open ourselves to inner guidance, connecting to our true self, our higher self, and to our Source.

Our Source can take on many facets and is within us. The Great Mother is a facet of that Source. She is available to help us create a new reality, one based in wholeness, love, ease and grace. One based in safety, freedom, fluidity and abundance.

But first we must open to her, align with her and listen.

This process can be challenging. At every turn we run into distractions and blocks. First, in the outer world and once that is silenced, in our inner world we are faced with our inner demons, if you will, our inner challenges.

I am facing a turning point on my path. This level of stillness at one point in my life sent me into therapy and, eventually, into treatment to face my past and to begin the healing process. But now I come on a restorative journey and quest, not a crisis. And I face the stillness and the quiet once again.

I open to go deeper as past traumas continue to heal and the awakened Self leads and anchors. I open to hear my inner guidance more clearly. I open to the wisdom of my body. I open to understand the signs better. I open to a refinement of my skills. I open to refine my gift of manifestation. I open to align more greatly with the Great Mother. To be infused by her, to live her, breathe her, and unite with her.

We are all on this path. It requires discipline at different intervals. I can use distractions, putting other things and people first. Why?, because it's kind of boring. It's kind of boring to have this intimate relationship with the Mother that requires stillness and not so much fanfare. There is a lot of stimuli in the spiritual and healing realm these days that it's easy to develop an ego around it.

It can be challenging to know and live the truth. I believe that's why questing is really important. Probably that's why we did it historically -- going out in nature to spend time with Spirit to clear the blocks and renew the connection.

The distractions and blocks are like the thoughts that rise in meditation. You learn to notice them and observe them and let them pass without attaching or judging. Staying focused on your intention, vision or mantra aligns you and moves you forward.

So I come to understand that refining my skills, connecting with Source really doesn't require a lot, just my openness.

"That's it. That's what I want you to tell them. Pray and meditate so that we can develop a connection and a relationship. Not to punish you or get you to be still simply for the sake of being still. No it's so that you can feel me and hear me and be nourished by my love and guidance."

God, it's really so simple.

It's not that old traditional religious dogma or all that "new age" stuff. Its right here – over and over the message is

"I am right here, LET ME IN, YOU ARE LOVED."

I am becoming comfortable with the quiet and the calm. I am surrendering. I am unveiling. I am revealing myself. I am pouring out of all my spaces and inhabiting all still space. I am reclaiming space. I am reclaiming this space here on earth. I am living freely. I am breathing fully. I am stretching out. I am resting. I am dancing. I am creating. I am FREE.

Eden is Everywhere

When we get out of the way and clear the pain and fear, we see that really Eden is everywhere.

The sacred is everywhere -- It is what you make of it. In the city, in the hills, it's everywhere.

Heaven is within, therefore, heaven is everywhere.

And the beauty of it is that there is nothing to do. You don't have to do anything to receive it, just open to receive it.

"My universe is gentle, kind and all loving. Enjoy all of its graces and gifts.

Play and create as a child in absolute trust and abandon.

Dare to dance and sing."

This universe is sustained by the Mother and there is more than enough. It is an abundant universe – Diverse, infinite, allowing.

She holds us and infuses her love into us at a cellular level. There is no limit to her love. She contains and holds this love, which manifests to meet all our needs.

"The nature of the universe is joy, play, creation.

You've heard of the Garden of Eden. It is REAL.

And it is right HERE. Open your eyes. Open your senses. You are living in it."

All Things Are Possible

As I close my quest of 2007 at Warner Hot Springs I recall all the stages of the journey that have led to this moment. To be here and journeyed, rested, cleared and played, and to do this with Mother/Father and my guides, without a financial strain, again this is testimony that all things are indeed possible. I recall that at the end of my journey in Crete, I felt such a call to give back and to learn the healing arts. And that's exactly what happened. I ended up at Agape International Spiritual Center at the Well Being Ministry, giving back and absorbing all forms of healing modalities. All Things Are Possible.

Today I feel filled by the Mother/Father and no longer seek anything because I am fueled from within. The great divine feminine/masculine energies are infused in me like the mineral springs of Warner Spring, like a water spout from the depth of the earth constantly giving its waters. The Great Divine Mother/Father is a wellspring within me, constantly pouring itself in me. Renewing me daily, moment by moment. I can experience the most intense emotional cycle, mental challenge, or physical imbalance, and then Universal Life Force, the Divine Mother/Father comes through me and reminds me of its presence in me and around me. It is my source of all, and it takes all forms, it manifests in the world through me and in my life.

My responsibility is to keep the channels open through my daily prayer and meditation my body/mind practices yoga, tai chi, meditation, etc. Through these practices I clear old energies, thoughts, ideas, feelings, behaviors, and toxins from the body, etc. keeping the channels open for new energy to come in, just like the earth does. It's a perfectly created organism and system that naturally cleanses and clears and renews and creates. It's a beautiful prism of energy flowing easily and perfectly in a sacred dance.

The Divine Mother/Father and my guides tell me to remain open .

I am always connected, never separate from them. That I need to rest in their security. And again to keep my channels open to more easily hear them and act accordingly. It becomes a perfect effortless, fluid dance.

"You will hear us more clearly," they tell me. "Just take a step back and listen to us when you have a question. Take a break take a minute, allow yourself the space from anyone or anything in order to act and respond according to your highest good. You will be guided; there is nothing that needs to rush you. Not even yourself. Utilize the sacred tools we have given you and that you have refined over the centuries. Enjoy them."

As I return, I do so with ease and grace, affirming that there will be more rest and abundance. And I know that my very being is service. That through living well, in a state of rest in the divine, I am of service to everyone I encounter. It is my commitment to enjoy and to rest in the Mother/Father. There is no separation. It is all One.

♥

Strengthening Our Connection

It's amazing how connected to the Divine Mother/Father I can be, and then outer events occur that challenge that connection. And I feel it's this old sense of rejection. I wonder how early I felt this disconnection, this pain, and then ultimately disconnected from my Source. Those relational injuries simply represent our disconnection with ourselves and the divine, our true Source within. We can experience wounding on the heart level by parents or close relations and friends which lead us to cut off our supply, our connection on the heart level. Yet all along, this connection is our main way of being in the flow, being in grace.

It is for this reason when our hearts are wounded through relationships it is crucial to heal, to take the time to process the experience, and to forgive. It is through this process that the heart stays open and receptive for the gifts of life, and it is in this way that pure love continues to flow through us and attracts more love.

The funny thing is that the love of our guides and Spirit is not conditional as is that of our fellow beings. They don't have issues with us, they are pure love and light. That's why children and animals see the Spirit realm so much easier, because they are pure love.

While on my quest in Warner Springs, I experienced the angelic realm more strongly then I have in a long time.

On my quest when I began to doubt my work and its viability in the world, an angel came down the path and completely interrupted and intercepted my thought. It enveloped me in its wings and I felt this wave and rush of energy that is difficult to describe because it is not of this realm. It was as if all the benefits I receive from my personal healing work and treatments manifested with this split second encounter from the angelic realm.

The Mother tells us that her angels and guides are all around us. We have just shut ourselves off from what is always here. Some people have an innate gift and see the angelic and higher realms easily. Most of us have cut this soul connection off due to our programming and how we relate to others.

But these realms are here and all around us. They love us as the Mother loves us. They are extensions of her light and their presence is getting stronger, entering our consciousness. And as they do, old debris must emerge and clear, which it will. That is all old experiences or cobwebs will be cleared. Not only within our own psyche, but also in the spaces we inhabit. As light comes in, all the old rancid energies and lower energies come out and go through a cycle of transmutation. Subsequently our connection to the divine strengthens. We are supported by divine realms and supported on our journey. Nothing is done of our own will, it is through this connection that all is done and realized.

The Divine Moves In All Places

I am in deep meditation this morning and as I enter I feel the Christ light and Mother's divine love pouring out into the grid of Los Angeles permeating the city at a deep level. I am becoming more and more aware of the new energy coming into this plane.

I am told that this energy is everywhere and being infused into this plane through the guides and beings of light that are assisting us at this time. I am told that people will be affected in inexplicable ways, that they will start changing and shifting and won't even know why they are doing it. My guides show me that the energy will carry and soothe people in ways they can't explain, it will move into all the nooks and crannies of their beings and cleans and clear them and cradle their wounds. This will occur at different intervals during this time of planetary shift.

They tell me and show me that this energy will move to all the impoverished areas and down hearted. To the homeless, the mentally ill, the physically impaired. Like a mist, it will wash over them and they won't understand why they feel different at peace or at ease. They tell me that this energy will also move to those attached to materialism, who are cut off from their true Source, and they, too, will begin behaving in unusual ways and their hearts will open. This energy will move into all areas -- to government officials and the rest of the world at large, like a mist that will permeate their cells and move into the darkest corners of the world and the universe. And it will comfort and heal and release many from bondage.

All the dark corners of the planet will be illuminated. This energy will move into all cultures of violence, abuse and misuse. It will move into the hearts, minds, and bodies of every man, woman, adolescent, and child, awakening higher consciousness. It will challenge all individuals around the world to awaken to consciousness, to choice. Each individual will begin to become more conscious of his or her thoughts, words and deeds. All will be healed and awakened.

The spark of God will awaken in the hearts and minds of all. As awareness emerges, the field of light and love strengthen on this plane. Any actions taken out of alignment with the divine will bring about quick results that create suffering. As a result, individuals around the world will seek new ways of living that are for the good of all. Individuals around the world will awaken to their God consciousness and begin to evolve.

This process can be felt now, next week, next year, or in 10 years. It is what is and it is what is here. It may be preceded by calamity and disaster both personal and global, but it is the Presence that washes over us all. As we are cracked open and our world and lives are turned upside down, the divine will pour itself in. Love and light will heal, guide, and inform us. It is for this reason that we are asked to keep our hearts open and commit to daily prayer and meditation. The more open our channels, the more able we are to feel and experience these infusions.

Our tendency is to focus on destruction and prepare for the fall of all systems. It is important, rather, to open our channels and receive inner guidance in order to move forward and create the new. This will come from within us. Open and receive.

Love and Receive Love

This morning in my meditation I heard, "It is not how much you earned today that matters, but rather, how you lived and loved." The idea is if money was not an issue and you had all the money you could ever need, what would you do, how would you be, how would you live?

Good questions.

The Mother tells us Love. Every minute, love. Don't judge, love. "Your brothers and sisters are all different and unique emanations of my Light, love them as yourself. See them as an extension of you. Remember you are one."

"I love you all equally," she tells us, "all of you with all of your weaknesses and challenges. My love for you has no limit, no bounds. I love you without condition."

Her love is pouring out like a blanket. It's like she has been aching to get really close to us and is utilizing every possible vessel to pour her energy into us. Waves are pouring forth like a blanket, a soft velvety blanket over the entire city, in fact the entire planet.

The Mother Supports All Men

Recently I shared with my partner how writing this book has impacted my awareness of the Source. That it is within me, all around me, and feminine. This has radically shifted my awareness of the Universe and my connection with it.

I shared how being born female in a male dominated culture cut me off from my source of life and my source of power and freedom. I shared how powerful it is to awaken to and realize that The Mother is also my source, that the universe is also my script in which I can manifest and create all I need, that through this awareness there is rest and ease and security because I rest in the presence of the Divine Mother that is one with me.

To my surprise he shared with me that he believes men have also suffered from the lack of awareness of God the Mother. He went on to say that all of us really suffer when there is an imbalance, untruth, or misrepresentation of the divine truth.

These words impacted me in a profound way. I know this truth but never fully grasped it. Yet right in front of me was a man telling me, you know, I have suffered too. And in hearing that, I saw how he has suffered. All of a sudden, I saw how his suffering is similar to the suffering I have endured over the years. I felt on all levels the truth and reality of this imbalance.

If the Mother sustains all of life and she has been underground for thousands of years, then not only has my life suffered as a result, but all have suffered. Men have suffered more than I think we could possibly imagine.

As the Mother returns and is seen and felt all around the world -- through many leaders and teachers, avatars and enlightened ones -- men begin to step forward and shed the old, embracing their bodies, their emotions, grieving their losses and releasing their pain, awakening to the new within themselves. And as they begin to embrace the Mother, they begin to open to her embrace, and to the feminine source within.

For it is the Mother that <u>sustains</u> all of life.

Open to her. She may rearrange a few things, but don't fear or worry. She carries you and sustains you. She transforms all darkness, all misalignment. She restores and renews and sustains. She holds all of you, your darkness and your light. She holds it, she soothes, she comforts, and she guides.

And one with her is the Father, the masculine spark within us all.

Open to Her, Open to Him. Open.

The Masculine in Balance with the Feminine

After a period of rest I was preparing to return to work and to the world. While walking in the Marina my attention was guided to the Star Wars images on the dumpsters along the peninsula. I recalled my conversation with my partner that morning. We had been talking about the effective use of energy and he noted how Star Wars had really brought that message out to the masses with its theme, "Use the Force Luke".

As I walked on this beautiful afternoon, I kept hearing 'Use the Force, Use the Force." I understood that it requires little effort, no effort really. I was reminded how the work was done simply by being, that people are affected more by presence than anything.

Well, that insight can be difficult to integrate. It seems my old ways of relating is in an old groove and I'm witnessing how I can overdo. I'm noticing how I get over involved and try to *do* the work, rather than allow it. It's a new level of awareness. Over the years it's been a process of removing myself from being over involved due to my up bringing in the classic female model, but now I'm challenged to back off even <u>more</u>.

So I ask for help from Mother/Father and their guides.

During my journey on the peninsula I was also shown the efficient use of yang energy. A group of women rowers were gliding on the water in perfect unison. Like the pelicans they moved with the rhythm of forward synchronized movement. When they changed the direction of the row, they chanted a three-word signal together and then collectively shifted their paddles to the other side and kept the rhythm going with their bodies. It was truly beautiful. I was being shown the efficient and excellent use of yang energy:

The flow in change, and the forward rhythm through change.

So I return to my work and bring with me new insight. I am now practicing the balance of yin and yang, anchored in rest and acting efficiently.

The world wants to disorient this sacred dance of masculine and feminine, yet it is the way. It is the natural way within us and in the universe. And it is beautiful.

The Father's Love is Limitless

The presence of the Divine Father comes through me as strongly as that of the Divine Mother. I believe it is all one. And yet there is a distinct quality that each brings. My experience with the Father began as a result of my being raised in a traditional religious paradigm. However, as I have healed and evolved, I still identify with and am connected to a presence that I experience as the Divine Father. This presence is often referred to as the Lord in Christian tradition as well as many other spiritual and religious paths.

The Father's love is limitless as the Mother's. He loves us beyond measure. Beyond our capacity to understand. His love is so great. He provides for us like a father does his child. He protects and showers us in limitless ways. His love is radiant and grand. To allow it in is to have the heart chakra explode wide open.

His love enables us to feel the strength within to move forward, to act and create in our world. It is the masculine energy of the universe, the yang principle that supports us in doing. The Father within, the masculine principle provides the rational, logical mind to balance and support the emotional, intuitive feminine principle. The balance and union of both principles allows us to create in harmony.

He tells us, "Let me in, I will do with you, I will provide all you need I will take care of all the details. My love for you is deep and great.

I have loved you since the moment you were conceived and before, and since. Let me love you my dear one, let me love you. Please open to me. There is nothing I want from you but that you open to me and know my love for you. All your needs are met. I find a way, sometimes quickly and sometimes slowly. I send you all the help you need. I love you my, dear one. I love you so tenderly and so loudly. I love you. Please let me.

I want to give to you infinitely. Please get out of the way.

Do you not know that I have always been here? Within you. You create so many distractions. You are so afraid to get quiet and still and even after you do, your chatter takes over and you worry and ruminate. But what you forgot long ago, and were taught to avoid is that I am the still small voice, I am the calm that washes over you for no apparent reason, I am the smile that shows up on a stranger's face, I am the deal that comes through for you, I am the peace that is beyond all measure in the center of your being. And I am waiting for you to Stop and Know Me."

"It's not a mystery. My love is real. It is simple and it is here. Open to me and let me in."

I feel this Divine Father, Buddha, Christ. I feel your love for me. I hear your voice telling me you want to provide all I need. I feel your love.

It is sometimes overwhelming to feel and then even more thrilling to see it unfold in this world. I see it unfold in a myriad of ways. Through my relationships, I feel your love coming through them. And sometimes through some out of the blue event.

Your love is great, real, true and constant. I realize this more and more. This love is not related to anything material, to getting this or that. To truly feel your love is to know that it is unlimited and beyond anything I could ever imagine wanting. It is a certainty and a security beyond any illusion that we create on this earth plane.

Sometimes there is an ebb and a stagnation in my outer world. I realize this is not a reflection of you or that life is testing me. Rather, that it is the nature of the universe to move in cycles: people and things change and shift.

As we are currently going through a planetary shift and everything is beginning to turn upside down and structures are dismantling. It is this Presence of God the Father and God the Mother that guides us through these changes and assists us in building a new world, one that is aligned to the divine. A world that is one in harmony with the feminine and masculine. No longer separate. All one.

As a young child, I learned all kinds of ways of dealing with others and the world around me. Part of that learning was to cut myself off from the Father and Mother, my very source, cutting myself from the flow of life and love. But today, I am learning to release those tendencies, and when I can't I receive loving guidance from healers and teachers that help me unblock those old patterns. I am then more able to remain in the flow of your love and the abundance of the universe. This is reality.

I remember as I was going through years of peeling the layers of stuff --.built-up pain, trauma, fear and resentment -- how you would speak to me and remind me of your presence. But those moments would pass so quickly because the waves of the past and the triggers of the present were so intense that they would take me under, and eventually I would lose the connection that was always there. But you kept at me, kept revealing yourself, and my guides did the same, edging me forward, challenging me to heal, pushing me to open, to release, to clear the debris and to move forward and into the world.

"My love for you has no condition. That is Love. It requires nothing, wants nothing, but to love and love fully.

I love you fully, and I am your source. Co-creating with you. I am within your very cells, I am your breath.

My love is limitless."

Have Trust and Faith in Me

"It's your job to be joyous and to let me take care of the details."

I feel you, Father, within me, beside me, around me. I feel your love for me, your tenderness and it's unlike any time I've experienced it before. It feels real and strong.

I feel your presence in a way that is tangible and palpable. I feel you there wanting to create with me. Every step and risk that I take out in the world you are there, meeting and greeting me. Just as a father does with a child. I sense my fear and my resistance, and you telling me, "Release the fear, I Am Here."

"You just need to take the step forward and I will greet you, and match you. Step out in faith and the universe will come and envelop you and match that faith and love."

It's amazing how many layers of trauma, fear, control, and barriers emerge challenging that trust. Yet all that we have worked through and have been building has now been anchored. We are challenged now to put down our resistance and trust the love in the universe, of the universe, that is the universe.

We are asked to step forward and let go, get out of the way, and allow the universe to gift us infinitely. We are told that the Divine Mother/Father and all our guides are at our side, doing overtime to put things together as the illusions and layers of our ego dissolve.

We are told that all of the old arises to be cleared. We are told not to fear it, but rather, to move through it. Face it, feel it, process it and move forward. Evolve. Evolve. Evolve.

It is Time.

Father's Day

Father's day is this week. Similarly to the Mother on Mother's Day, I feel the Father is present. It's interesting how the love is the same, but the energy is definitely more masculine. These experiences show me that there truly is a divine presence that is masculine and feminine. They are equal and the same, yet distinct and unique in their qualities. Each has a unique message for us. And yet they are one, here to tell us that it is within that we connect with them and it is from within that they provide all of our needs. All of them.

They come to tell us that they are loving and supporting us. They are our divine parents. Unlike our earthly parents, they are perfection. They meet all of our needs. They love us and know us and they are always listening and talking to us.

The presence of the Father is strong. He comes in the face of Christ, the Buddha, Muhammad, Krishna, etc. He comes to tell us that he is always with us and provides for all of our needs, that he and the army of beings of light are working on our behalf and guiding us on the journey.

"Open yourself to me, listen to me in your meditations, talk to me in your prayers...commune with me. I am right here by your side, within you. It is not a mystery, my love for you. It is unconditional and constant. I know your pain, your fears, your concerns. I hear you, and I listen. I love you. As your Father, I care for you and work on your behalf to meet all your needs, sending you all you need for your journey, assisting you through your lessons and your learning. My Love is deep and gentle.

I do not wish for you to suffer, there is no need for sacrifice -- that time has come to an end. It is time for you to live fully and joyfully. Listen to your inner guidance, trust yourself and trust me within you. Clear your mental and emotional body, and this can be done with prayer and meditation. Ask to have all that blocks you from joy be removed and lifted. Call on me and your guides. Utilize the energies of the divine. All is available at this time to lighten your load and to clear your path.

Rejoice my dear ones, rejoice the time has come and it is now."

In Prayer

It is Father's Day. The funny thing is I am feeling conflicted about this day. I feel the presence of the Father, however, I don't feel a lot of goodness when I think of some of our male leaders. I feel more a sense of disappointment. When I think of the men that lead our nations, our financial institutions, our technological world, I wonder where integrity and truth are.

I wonder where you are in our world Father.

I wonder why it takes so many cycles for the truth of who you are to manifest in our male leaders.

I wonder when the divine masculine will awaken and materialize fully on this plane.

I wonder when the true male paradigm will begin to emerge and live and breathe and lead this country and the world.

I wonder when mankind will begin to create out of responsibility, caring for its people and land.

I wonder when a man with an open heart will find the power and strength to lead men.

I wonder when we will allow this gentle man to emerge.

This is my prayer Father, it is my prayer that this consciousness arises today and awakens across the nation and ripples out into the world.

It is my prayer that I may be a vessel that nurtures that man.

It is my prayer that I be guided and taught how to nurture that man in my partner and all men on my path.

It is my prayer that I may heal from the wounding of the past and be given the clear vision of that man, supporting him as an enlightened woman that is also supported by him.

I pray that I heal and clear the past, allowing old energy to transmute into the new, the clean, the clear, the brilliant.

I open to the re-birth of the male species. I commit to hold that vision. To see it and feel it as it becomes reality.

(A year after this section was written Barack Obama was elected as President of the United States)

The Stillness of the Divine Masculine

We saw my partner's spiritual teacher today. There is something so basic and simple, yet so profound, about his teachings. It seems to satiate a thirst.

Today I felt his energy as that of a gentle enlightened man. I could see that he is, in fact, an enlightened master - a clear mind and an open heart. His vibration is very high, so simple. I've heard it said, enlightenment is simply becoming a true human being. I believe he is one who lives and walks in truth.

Today He spoke of quite a bit. Most of what he said I am still digesting. Most I just received vibrationally.

I'm sure I could've learned more by speaking, but something was happening to me that I can't quite describe. It's like I experienced a peace and joy unattached to anything.

It was the stillness of the divine masculine. A still mind - the beauty of a balanced rational and logical mind. An experience of the divine masculine principle. A glimpse into the possibility within us all, man and woman. The peace and beauty of the masculine in its rightful state. When the masculine within us, the rational mind finds its rest and stillness within – wow, there is a joy that cannot be described. It is brilliant.

♥ ♥

The Creation Process

Nature Teaches the Art of Being and Doing

When you witness and observe nature, you see the perfect balance of yin and yang. Being and doing. Stillness and action. The hills, brush, trees, and plant life are rooted in being. From the observers point of view there appears to be very little movement. They are the wise ones that teach us grounding and stillness.

We are then greeted by the movement of the winged and four-legged ones. The hummingbirds move about with great speed in work and play. Squirrels move through tree branches and ground holes, harvesting for the winter.

As I walk in the canyon, the ground beneath me and the trees above me teach me to be still. What perfect teachers. They teach me the strength in being. They nourish my body and bring me to a state of rest. As I climb, I feel the energy of the yang and observe life all around me, moving, creating, singing and dancing.

Doing is as beautiful as being when born out of rest. Then it becomes the joy of doing. Doing comes from Peace. *Doing comes from the breath of life, Mother/Father God, Universal Consciousness* which moves through you and expresses itself as you and through your creations. That is the beauty of doing.

It's All Energy

The universe is made of energy particles and waves. Creation is the alchemical reaction of energy. Positive and negative polarities moving into and out of each other, creating friction and movement and, then eventually, slowing down to create matter.

The most common form of energy that lives in the Universe is the energy of love. It is the unifying field. It is the glue of the Universe. It is the essence -- the divine nature of the Universe and the center of creation, the place in which the Mother and Father reside, and move and operate.

There are many other forces and forms of energy in the universe. All of which can be used to create. One can create from love, faith, oneness or fear, hate, anger, separation. It is truly a choice.

With which energy do you want to create? Which are you currently creating with?

All is Energy, and all energy is changing and renewing.

Energy is never destroyed. It is only transformed from one form to another. You have a choice to create with anger, fear, worry, grief etc. Or you can allow these forms of energy to transform and transmute into passion, faith, trust, creativity, etc.

All challenging emotions and thoughts are forms of energy, when allowed and when honored can have a space to transform and empower your life. Rather then being a victim of these emotions or thoughts, you can move into the truth that you are the creator of your world and you have choice.

Creation Dance

Creation is the sacred dance between the feminine and masculine principle. It is a fluid dance. It is within each of us.

It moves with ease and grace. Sometimes it is fiery. Sometimes it is still. For certain, it is incredibly beautiful.

The equal dance between the feminine and masculine principle, in each of us and between us.

It is the way of the new paradigm.

Creation is easy. It doesn't take a lot. Thought, word, emotion, deed. Sometimes instantly, sometimes slowly.

And creation is fun. Not hard work. Really. If we lean into that, it is easy, full, and abundant.

Our intention will manifest through our deliberate thought, and feeling states for our highest good. If it is not for our highest good, then it will not manifest. To create responsibly is to let go and accept this reality, self will has only created the destruction we are witnessing in our world.

So move on and go within to discover a renewed vision, that which comes from your truth and your connection to Source. It will manifest. If not now, then later. If not later, then something better.

"Vision, Intend, Act, and then... let go.

This is the creation dance, the co-creative dance."

This can sometimes be a very challenging process. Letting go and surrendering to the higher good can be painful at times. Loss of a relationship, a project or job, a spouse or child, or the lack of these things can bring about grief and suffering. Sometimes the will of the divine feels so out of alignment with our will that the co-creative dance feels like a tug of war instead of a dance.

I believe this process will either take us into despair, disconnecting us from ourselves, our fellows and our Source, or bring us to greater surrender and into greater awakening.

Oftentimes it takes personal challenge or tragedy to push us into a deeper awareness of who we are. We are forced to look to a higher source for guidance. This can lead to an awakening to the truth of who we are and our higher purpose. It is through such an awakening that we open to choice, the ability to create our reality, and divine will. No longer victims of circumstances, we realize that we are designed to heal and evolve. We are supported by an infinite source on an endless journey of creation.

"Create with an open heart, and let go of the results. It is all good, and it all leads to Love."

Live the Vision, Focus on the Vision

Live the vision. Stay focused on what you are creating. See it, feel it. This has been said in many ways over thousands of years. Live it now. Feel it now. It is simple, really.

When yin and yang energy are balanced it is easier to focus on your vision and effectively manifest it in the physical realm.

By being in a receptive space, at rest and opening, you can receive the higher vision from your Higher Self (your true essence, your inner self) and your union with Spirit. It is important to receive it and give it a period of time to steep, hold, anchor within your psyche. Hold the space to allow the vision to clarify, and set the motion and direction. Once the vision is clear and guidance and direction arises from within, the action to manifest the vision naturally arises.

A period of being with and clarifying your vision, allowing actions to arise from it, is crucial in order to allow the vision to anchor. Otherwise you are stuck in a spin cycle and being run around in circles by your visions.

Don't be discouraged when your vision takes time to manifest. Allow the tides to pass, the storms of the universe to rearrange some things to create your higher purpose and meet your needs. Know that what ever does not materialize may either be replaced with something better or may not be quite ready to give birth.

Trust and have faith in the infinite possibilities. Some visions take longer than others to manifest. This does not negate the reality that you are deeply loved and cared for by a loving presence that is always with you and takes on many forms, known as angels or beings of Light. This loving presence moves in and through friends, family, even strangers.

Open yourself to receive even in those places of greatest doubt and adversity. Believe, believe in the goodness.

We are living in times where so much of the old and the decayed is emerging to be cleared. Sometimes this can fog the lens and create an illusion of reality. Do not attach to this illusion, look beyond it.

"See it as clearing the painful events of your world. They come up to be cleared and transmuted. The Light and Love in all beings is strengthening and intensifying so the ego struggles to release itself, and like the death process, makes its last attempts to run the show before releasing and transmuting into its new life.

See it through. Believe."

Balance/Wholeness

I have been shown that when I spend time in yin and really steep in rest, taking in the gifts of the universe and its abundance, then when it is time to do and be active in the world, it is effortless and joyous.

This is a result of operating from wholeness. When I am operating from being, from rest, from absolute trust and abandon in my connection to the Mother/Father and the universe, I am full. Doing comes from this space.

When I operate from stagnation and depletion, I am in unbalanced masculine energy and operate from fear and worry and mistrust of the universe, therefore my paint strokes come out distorted and there is a lot of hit and miss.

But when the feminine and masculine energy within me is balanced and I am in harmony in body, mind and spirit, then my actions are precise, flowing and refined. So simple, not necessarily easy, yet so beautiful.

Mother Father God

"We are one, the great yin/yang. We call you at this time to share with you the glory of the multidimensional reality that exists within you and all around you. We speak to you directly, shattering all old paradigms as they transmute into renewed paths of freedom, based in truth, equality, love and peace.

The time for your planet's evolutionary shift is now, and all are being called back home, within.

Trust in the divine in all matters and in all affairs, put all your trust within, not in people or circumstances. Those will shift and change like the tides. We are constant, always listening and guiding. You will receive all you need. As you let go of attachments, all that you need in people, places, and things will be provided.

Put your full trust in us and the rest will follow. Commit to not worrying. It is a waste of energy. At this time, all energy is needed to rebuild your world. A renewed world, unlike any you've ever known. Open, receive, let the good in."

Closing

As I conclude these writings, I rest here at The Healing Center, which is devoted to the Divine Mother and to the healing and awakening of individuals and the collective. My business partner, Luciana, and I attained this space a little over a year ago. It is a space for rest, a place of healing, one of many healing centers around the world that is birthing a new world, honoring the feminine, the body, and the healing arts.

What a gift to be a part of such a large community of light workers as we co-create this dance of the divine on this earth plane.

So much has yet to unfold. Beauty and harmony. The creative principles of the universe are coming together. Feminine and masculine. Body, mind and spirit in harmony, balance, and equality.

Much is shedding now in our world. It's a bit rocky at times. Unnerving at others. But this shedding has been foretold by thousands, this end of days, this birth of a new consciousness. The planet earth is shifting and the entire universe is evolving.

How beautiful, and how magnificent.

Mother and Father, the yin and yang, the divine, the great oneness, speaks within each of us and all around us.

"Open the line of communication between you and your Source -- whatever shape that takes for you. Open the line of communication between you and your brothers and sisters with compassion and understanding. Bring order to your affairs. And live.

Live my dear ones.

Live.

Love.

And Give.

Shed the old, embrace your body, honor your emotions and allow the pain and anger to heal. Forgive yourself, forgive others. Allow your mind to still in the presence of the divine within you and rest your soul in the arms and bosom of the Divine Mother/Father, rest my dear ones. All is well."

All are Loved

♥

There is no punishment

There is no other

There is only love

And love sees all and holds all

The darkest of corners, the darkest heart is loved

Love is limitless, it knows no time or space.

It takes the darkest acts and turns them into beauty.

Every being on this planet and in this universe is loved without condition. This is not sentimental love nor romantic love, this is divine love.

This love guides all towards the light, through its cycles of shedding barriers.

As the soul opens, the love comes through and reawakens the light within.

The Divine Mother/Father tells us "We are with you always in all ways. No conditions, no limits."

All are Loved.

9 780578 031330